MW00932648

WORKBOOK FOR BJ FOGG'S "TINY HABITS"

OAK TREE READING

Copyright © 2022 Oak Tree Reading All rights reserved

No part of this book may be reproduced, or stored in a retrieval system, or transmitted in any form or by any means, electronic, mechanical, photocopying, recording, or otherwise, without express written permission of the publisher.

ISBN 9798427126137

Independently published

Cover design by: Oak Tree Reading

Printed in the United States of America

Contents

Welcome to a Better Reading Experience

This workbook is specifically designed to optimize your learning.

By completing this workbook, you will get more value from the books you read. You will be able to easily implement the knowledge and guidance shared by authors. As a result, you will see the positive impact books start to have on your life. And most importantly, you will enjoy reading more than ever before.

Why use a workbook while you read?

When we read, we are engaging in passive learning. This type of learning results in very little retention and almost no long-term benefits. In our fast-paced, time-scarce culture we rush through books, but ironically this wastes more time, as it is almost like you never read the book to begin with.

This workbook helps you engage in **active learning**. Active learning involves participating in the learning process in some way – by writing, speaking, or doing. The more ways we engage with what we are learning, the more likely we are to remember it long-term. Even better, when you are involved in discussions with others about what you read, your retention improves further.

Lastly, you will always have this workbook available to you for an easy refresher course on the book once it's all filled out.

Here's what is included in your workbook:

- Pre-reading questions
- All discussion questions with space for writing answers
- Space to write your own summary for each chapter
- Vocabulary with space to write definitions and add words
- Key terms with space to write definitions
- Chapter reflection questions
- Final reflection questions
- A condensed list of all discussion questions and vocabulary.
- Reflection pages for writing extra notes and ideas

How to Use the Workbook

Fill out the pre-reading questions before you read.

Get in the right headspace before you start reading. Reflect on your answers each time you read.

Read each section before working on the discussion questions.

Test your retention then go back and find the answers you can't remember. This trains your brain to remember more while you read.

Do the reflection questions.

These questions reinforce *why* you want to remember what you learned. Your brain will only remember information it thinks is relevant or important. Your job is to tell it why that is.

Return to what you wrote.

Repetition is a key to learning. Re-reading the answers you wrote a day later is a simple and very effective way to remember the material long-term.

Using this Workbook in a Group Setting

Having a reading buddy or group can be very helpful! It makes reading more fun, easily allows you to engage in the learning process, and a friend or colleague can be a great accountability partner. Let's talk about some helpful tips for using discussion questions in different group settings

Reading with Friends

Read on your own first. Becoming familiar with the material will make time spent discussing it with others much more effective.

Set goals together. Make sure you are on the same page about how much you will read and in what timeframe.

Have a plan. With busy schedules and hectic lives, committing to a regular time to meet together and discuss what you read is the only way the best of intentions aren't thwarted by life's demands.

Check-in regularly. Don't just meet up at the end of the book and expect to be able to go through the entire workbook in one sitting. Whether it's weekly, monthly or something else, find what works for you.

Talk about how you will implement what you've learned. Talking to someone about how and why you want to use the tools or information you have learned will help you not only figure out the best way to do it, but they can also help keep you on track and provide encouragement.

Be respectful. No one sees things the same way. We can learn from each other's different viewpoints. Make the discussion a safe space for sharing thoughts and ideas. If people are worried about sounding dumb or being wrong, they won't open up and you'll being doing a disservice to them and to yourself.

Reading with a Book Club

Have a plan. When you are reading with a group it is imperative you start with a plan. I recommend creating a plan for the entire book from the start. Having a set timeline and schedule will make coordination with many people much easier.

Talk about your "why". Before you begin reading, schedule a time to get together to talk about what you want to learn from the book. Discussing this with others can spark ideas, inspiration and motivation.

Divvy up the responsibility. Whether one person facilitates an entire meeting, or each person is given a chapter or section, giving someone the role of running things will help things go smoothly and take the burden off of one person. The benefit is twofold - everyone is actively engaged, and the variety will provide different perspectives and insight.

Be flexible, but stay on purpose long-term. Things never go exactly as planned when other people are involved. When this happens try not to stress out, just go with the flow. If it becomes a weekly occurrence however, it may be a good time to have another discussion about goals and why you all want to meet in the first place.

Reading With a Work Team

Get on the same page. There is likely some reason someone thought it was a good idea for your team to read this book. What is the purpose of reading this book specifically? What are your team goals? Do not start reading until you have all agreed upon this.

Set a schedule. This may be easier or more challenging depending on your work environment. Figuring out a regular time everyone can commit to is a must if you want to make the most reading together.

Set expectations. You don't want your meeting to feel controlled or contrived, but likely the meeting times are going to be shorter than a regular book club, with less time for chit-chat. Decide as a team what each person is responsible for before the meeting, during the meeting, and after the meeting. Decide what will be discussed in the meeting and what will not.

Review and adjust. After your first 3 or so meetings, take some time to discuss how everyone is feeling about the meetings. What is going well? What needs to be improved? Using a "start doing, stop doing, do more of, do less of" diagram can be very helpful for this exercise. It may also be necessary to do follow-ups until your team is happy with the process and results.

Be accountable and encouraging. You have all decided it is a good idea to read this book and that it will benefit the team as a whole and each of the members individually. Now it's time to see it in action. When you see a team member engaging in the new thing they have learned, be supportive and cheer them on. Change is hard. Having others to support you can be the difference in changing or falling back into familiar habits.

Tips for Teachers

Individual work is important, too. It is tempting to lecture straight through the material or dive right into discussions, but the way to have thoughtful, meaningful discussions is by giving students time to first read and gather their thoughts on their own.

Utilize small groups. Facilitating a discussion with 30 people (or more) can be a nightmare. Instead set up some small groups with a guided activity. Afterwards, if you think it would be helpful, send up a representative from each group to share what they discussed with the class.

Shuffle. Have people engage with different people, especially if the class is all day long or lasts for multiple sessions. This allows students an opportunity to be exposed to different perspectives and voices.

Don't try and get through everything. If you have 50 minutes, don't push your class to get through as much as possible. This takes away from the value of the questions and the ability to have an open platform for discussion. It becomes a trivial exercise in finding the answers then immediately forgetting them as soon as you walk out of the room.

Encourage collaboration outside the classroom. Ask students to work in pairs to come up with ideas on how they will apply the information they learned. There are any number of creative ways to encourage students to practice what they've learned, try out a couple ideas and see what you like best.

Oak Tree Reading Workbook

Tiny Habits

BJ Fogg

Pre-Reading Questions

What initially made you interested in this book? Did someone recommend it to you?

Read the publisher's summary either on the book itself or on the webpage where you purchased it. What appears to be the main idea or purpose of this book?

What are you hoping to gain from this book?

Will this book help you enhance some area of your life? Work, school, home, personal?

If you implement what the tools, strategies, or knowledge taught in the book, how do you see it being able to positively impact your life?

Jot down any other thoughts you have before you begin reading.

Oak Tree Reading Workbook

Tiny Habits

BJ Fogg

Introduction Chapter

Chapter Questions

What cultural message do we internalize about change?

What is flawed in our approach to change?

What does popular thinking about habit formation lead to?

What three things should you do to design successful habits?

What does not reliably change behavior on its own? What is the name of this fallacy?

In what three ways can we create lasting change?

How does the scarcity mindset affect our ability to change?

Describe the Maui Habit.

How does risk impact our ability to change?

How does our aspiration culture negatively impact our ability to change?

Which two components of behavioral change are unreliable?

What is a key maxim of Behavior design?

What does celebrating small successes teach you how to do?

What is the anatomy of Tiny Habits?

Vocabulary

Iterate

_____:

_____:

Key Terms

ABCs of Tiny Habits:

_____:

Chapter Summary In few sentences, describe the main concepts from the chapter.

Oak Tree Reading Workbook

Tiny Habits

BJ Fogg

Chapter 1: _____

Chapter Questions

What are the three elements of behavior?

What is motivation?

What is ability?

What is a prompt?

Draw the Fogg Behavioral Model graph.

What happens when a behavior is prompted above the Action Line?

What combination causes a behavior to be above or the below the Action Line?

Where do habits fall on the Fogg Behavioral Model?

When will people do a behavior if motivation is middling?

What makes you less likely to do a behavior?

How do motivation and ability work together?

How does repetition affect behavior?

What does it mean to say motivation and ability are "continuous variables?"

How can you disrupt a behavior?

What is the rule of reciprocity?

What are the three steps for troubleshooting a behavior?

What are the two purposes of observing the world with a Behavior Model lens?

In which two scientific ways should you examine your own behavior?

What does the Motivation Monkey do?

Vocabulary

Dubious:

Referendum:

_____:

_____:

Key Terms

Fogg Behavioral Model:

B=MAP:

Action Line:

Motivation:

Ability:

Prompt:

_____:

_____:

Chapter Summary In few sentences, describe the main concepts from the chapter.

Reflection Questions

What did you find the most interesting in this chapter?

How does the material in this chapter relate to any of your current life experiences or situations?

What can you take away from this chapter to implement into that situation or future relevant experiences?

Was there anything that confused you or that you would like to know more about?

Was there anything you disagreed with? How would you approach it differently?

Reflections Page

Use this space for anything that comes to you as you read. It can be notes, quotes, feelings, experiences, drawings, charts, etc.

Chapter Questions

What two words are indicators that you are relying on motivation to drive change?

What are the three sources of motivation?

What are the four elements of motivation that make it hard to control?

Why is motivation unreliable?

Why don't aspirations yield results?

What is the difference between aspirations, outcomes, and behaviors?

When can you achieve aspirations and outcomes?

What does the term "goal" usually indicate?

Draw the Swarm of Behaviors tool.

What question do you ask when creating a Swarm of Behaviors chart?

What are the three ways NOT to find your best habit?

What are the three steps in Behavior Design?

What are the criteria of a Golden Behavior?

Draw a Focus Map grid.

What question is asked during the first round of focus mapping?

What question is asked during the second round of focus mapping?

What distinction can help you avoid judgement during the second round of focus mapping?

What is Fogg Maxim #1?

What is the purpose of a Focus Map?

What is the last step of Focus Mapping?

What should you think about your new habits as?

Vocabulary

_____:

_____:

Key Terms

PAC

Swarm of Behaviors

Magic Wanding

Golden Behavior

Focus Map

Fogg Maxim #1

_____:

_____:

Chapter Summary In few sentences, describe the main concepts from the chapter.

Reflection Questions

What did you find the most interesting in this chapter?

How does the material in this chapter relate to any of your current life experiences or situations?

What can you take away from this chapter to implement into that situation or future relevant experiences?

Was there anything that confused you or that you would like to know more about?

Was there anything you disagreed with? How would you approach it differently?

Reflections Page

Use this space for anything that comes to you as you read. It can be notes, quotes, feelings, experiences, drawings, charts, etc.

Oak Tree Reading Workbook

Tiny Habits

BJ Fogg

Chapter 3: _____

Chapter Questions

What assumption do most people operate under?

Why are small changes better than big changes?

What are the drawbacks of attempting big changes?

What is the "burst and bust" cycle?

What are the 4 steps in Behavior Design?

Why do we want to make behaviors easy to do?

How does ability affect behavior on the Behavioral Model graph?

When you design a new habit, what are you designing for?

What question should you always start with when creating a new habit? What is the name for this question?

What are the 5 ability factors?

Why is the Ability Chain a transformative tool?

What makes a habit design unstable?

What is the Breakthrough Question?

What three things make behaviors easier to do?

What is "skilling up"?

When should you engage in skilling up?

What is decision fatigue?

What are the two ways to make a habit tiny?

What is the objective of the Starter Step?

What is an important part of the Tiny Habits mindset?

Why does the Starter Step have a big impact?

What is Scaling Back?

How do you determine which step you should start with?

What are the four questions in the Design Flow?

How do you keep a habit alive?

What feelings are a sign that your habit is not tiny enough?

What is important to remember about procrastination?

Vocabulary

_____:

_____:

Key Terms

Discovery Question:

Breakthrough Question:

Starter Step:

Scaling Back:

_____:

_____:

Chapter Summary In few sentences, describe the main concepts from the chapter.

Reflection Questions

What did you find the most interesting in this chapter?

How does the material in this chapter relate to any of your current life experiences or situations?

What can you take away from this chapter to implement into that situation or future relevant experiences?

Was there anything that confused you or that you would like to know more about?

Was there anything you disagreed with? How would you approach it differently?

Reflections Page

Use this space for anything that comes to you as you read. It can be notes, quotes, feelings, experiences, drawings, charts, etc.

Oak Tree Reading Workbook

Tiny Habits

BJ Fogg

Chapter 4: _____

Chapter Questions

What is crucial to know about the effect of prompts on behavior?

What makes prompts an invisible driver of behavior?

What are the 5 steps in behavior design?

What two things will keep a behavior from happening?

Why don't many prompts work?

What are the three types of prompts?

Why do person prompts often not work?

What is a context prompt?

What kind of behaviors are context prompts best suited for?

If a prompt is not working, what should you do and not do?

What is an action prompt?

What type of prompt is the most useful?

What is an Anchor?

What is behavior sequencing?

What creates a reliable habit?

What is the Tiny Habit Recipe?

List a few examples of anchors.

What three things should you take into account when looking for a good anchor?

Why is experimentation important in habit design?

What is a Trailing Edge?

What is a Meanwhile Habit?

What is a Pearl Habit?

How can a pearl habit help in situations where we feel powerless?

How do people change best?

Vocabulary

Behest:

Forebode:

Profuse:

_____:

_____:

Key Terms

Person Prompt:

Context Prompt:

Action Prompt:

Anchor:

Tiny Habit Recipe:

Trailing Edge:

_____:

_____:

Chapter Summary In few sentences, describe the main concepts from the chapter.

Reflection Questions

What did you find the most interesting in this chapter?

How does the material in this chapter relate to any of your current life experiences or situations?

What can you take away from this chapter to implement into that situation or future relevant experiences?

Was there anything that confused you or that you would like to know more about?

Was there anything you disagreed with? How would you approach it differently?

Reflections Page

Use this space for anything that comes to you as you read. It can be notes, quotes, feelings, experiences, drawings, charts, etc.

Oak Tree Reading Workbook

Tiny Habits

BJ Fogg

Chapter 5: _____

Chapter Questions

What do adults rarely do?

What results from celebrating the Tiny Habits way?

What two things define what celebration is?

Why is celebration an important element of behavioral change?

How does effective celebration affect the brain?

How does celebration correlate with learning?

What is the psychological definition of learning?

What reinforces behavior?

Aside from positive feelings, what is another type of positive experience?

What is the relationship between dopamine and good feelings?

What is reward prediction error?

How do celebrations hack the reward prediction error?

What is directly connected to how you feel when you do a behavior?

How quickly can habits form when connected to strong positive emotions?

What creates habits?

What is the Spectrum of Automaticity?

What causes a behavior to become more automatic each time you do it?

What is the definition of a reward?

When do rewards need to occur?

What types of rewards are unhelpful when trying to create a new habit?

What two factors are the dopamine reward reaction dependent on?

What is Fogg Maxim #2?

What are the 2 steps to help a habit root quickly?

What will occur if your celebration feels phony?

What is Shine?

What is a Power Celebration?

What are the three reasons you should celebrate after doing a tiny habit?

What may be happening if you feel celebrating small stuff is hard for you?

Why can digging deep help you discover the value of celebrating?

What is the purpose of lowering your expectations?

List a few strategies for cultivating the feeling of success.

What is the fastest way to wire in a new habit?

What two things are you training when you rehearse your tiny habits?

What are the three times to celebrate a tiny habit?

After you develop a habit, under what circumstances should you reimplement celebrations?

What will cause your brain to rewire a habit to want to avoid it?

What is the benefit of engaging in unplanned celebrations?

Why do celebrations affect confidence?

What is a celebration blitz?

Vocabulary

Berate:

Pragmatic:

_____:

_____:

Key Terms

Spectrum of Automaticity:

Fogg Maxim #2:

Shine:

Power Celebration:

_____:

_____:

Chapter Summary In few sentences, describe the main concepts from the chapter.

Reflection Questions

What did you find the most interesting in this chapter?

How does the material in this chapter relate to any of your current life experiences or situations?

What can you take away from this chapter to implement into that situation or future relevant experiences?

Was there anything that confused you or that you would like to know more about?

Was there anything you disagreed with? How would you approach it differently?

Reflections Page

Use this space for anything that comes to you as you read. It can be notes, quotes, feelings, experiences, drawings, charts, etc.

Oak Tree Reading Workbook

Tiny Habits

BJ Fogg

Chapter 6: _____

Chapter Questions

Describe the garden metaphor for habits.

How long does it take for habits to grow to their full expression?

What three things does habit formation time depend on?

What determines how difficult it is to form a habit?

What are the two general categories of habits?

Describe an example of a growing habit.

What is the limitation of growing habits?

What does a multiplying habit look like?

What role do aspirations play in creating growth and multiplication habits?

What doesn't matter very much in terms of success?

What can happen when fear is removed?

How do demotivators affect habits?

Why is the first time you do a behavior critical?

When can people do harder behaviors?

How do you acquire the skills of change?

What are the three steps of Behavior Crafting?

What skill helps you go from tiny to transformative?

What are three guidelines for behavior crafting?

How will you feel when you are doing the right thing?

What are the two components of Self-Insight?

What are the three guidelines for self-insight?

What kind of change should you look for?

What three skills are associated with Process Skills?

What is the Process Skill?

What moves your comfort edge?

List the 4 guidelines for adjusting the difficulty of a habit.

Why are Context Skills important to develop?

What is the Context Skill?

What two questions guide you for developing context skills?

What are the 4 guidelines for Context Skills?

What are 4 skills associated with Mindset Skills?

What is the Mindset Skill?

What deeply rooted human drive can help cultivate habits?

Write some examples of ways to utilize the Mindset Skill.

List the 5 Skills of Change.

Vocabulary

_____:

_____:

Key Terms

Growth Habit:

Multiplication Habit:

Behavior Crafting:

Self-Insight:

Process Skill:

Context Skill:

Mindset Skill:

_____:

_____:

Chapter Summary In few sentences, describe the main concepts from the chapter.

Reflection Questions

What did you find the most interesting in this chapter?

How does the material in this chapter relate to any of your current life experiences or situations?

What can you take away from this chapter to implement into that situation or future relevant experiences?

Was there anything that confused you or that you would like to know more about?

Was there anything you disagreed with? How would you approach it differently?

Reflections Page

Use this space for anything that comes to you as you read. It can be notes, quotes, feelings, experiences, drawings, charts, etc.

Oak Tree Reading Workbook

Tiny Habits

BJ Fogg

Chapter 7: _____

Chapter Questions

Name and define the three categories of habits.

What language isn't helpful for changing bad habits?

What is a better analogy for changing bad habits?

Why does the inability to stop a habit cause shame?

List the three steps in the Behavioral Change Masterplan.

What type of habit should you focus on in Phase #1 and why?

What is the benefit of starting with creating new behaviors first?

What are the three components of a habit you can alter to stop a behavior?

What is a common mistake when trying to stop a bad habit?

Which of your specific habits should you start with when working towards changing a general habit?

What are the three ways to address the prompt of a habit in order to stop a behavior?

List the 5 factors in the Ability Chain and how you can use each of them in your favor to stop a habit.

Why is starting with motivation a mistake when trying to stop a habit?

What are the two options for decreasing motivation to stop a habit?

What is a demotivator?

What are the drawbacks to using demotivators?

List the 4 ways you can scale back a change.

Why does scaling back work?

What will cause habit swapping to fail?

What is prompt remapping?

What can help if you find yourself forgetting to do the new habit?

What visual aid can help you while designing a habit swap?

What are the four options for swapping a habit?

What are some options to try if your habit swap isn't working?

What are habits of omission?

Vocabulary

Nefarious:

_____:

_____:

Key Terms

_____:

_____:

Chapter Summary In few sentences, describe the main concepts from the chapter.

Reflection Questions

What did you find the most interesting in this chapter?

How does the material in this chapter relate to any of your current life experiences or situations?

What can you take away from this chapter to implement into that situation or future relevant experiences?

Was there anything that confused you or that you would like to know more about?

Was there anything you disagreed with? How would you approach it differently?

Reflections Page

Use this space for anything that comes to you as you read. It can be notes, quotes, feelings, experiences, drawings, charts, etc.

Oak Tree Reading Workbook

Tiny Habits

BJ Fogg

Chapter 8: _____

Chapter Questions

What is a powerful driver of behavior?

Why is it important to get cooperation when you are designing change?

What maxim helps influence others to change their behaviors?

What can open other people up to new types of change?

When are we influencing the behavior of others?

What makes change harder for others in the future?

What two things must you do in order to help others change?

What are the two approaches for getting others to change?

What is the first step in designing change in a group?

What is the second step in designing change in a group?

What is the objective of the second step?

Describe the process as a Ringleader for finding golden behaviors.

Which question should the Ninja use for step 3?

What is step 4 for designing change in a group?

What question should a ringleader ask in step 4?

In step 5, who should you talk to in order to find out what is successfully prompting a target behavior?

What method helps other people feel successful?

When should we offer positive feedback?

What should we look for in response to giving positive feedback?

When does feedback have the most emotional power?

What should a ringleader do in step 7?

Under what 4 categories can people fall when you are trying to design a behavioral change?

What group(s) should you focus on and what group(s) should you not spend time on?

What do innovators often do wrong with respect to these 4 groups?

Vocabulary

Intractable:

Perpetuate:

_____:

_____:

Key Terms

_____:

_____:

Chapter Summary In few sentences, describe the main concepts from the chapter.

Reflection Questions

What did you find the most interesting in this chapter?

How does the material in this chapter relate to any of your current life experiences or situations?

What can you take away from this chapter to implement into that situation or future relevant experiences?

Was there anything that confused you or that you would like to know more about?

Was there anything you disagreed with? How would you approach it differently?

Reflections Page

Use this space for anything that comes to you as you read. It can be notes, quotes, feelings, experiences, drawings, charts, etc.

Oak Tree Reading Workbook

Tiny Habits

BJ Fogg

Final Reflection Questions

What part(s) of this book did you enjoy the most? Why?

What part(s) of this book did you dislike? Why?

What are your top 3 key takeaways from this book?

How will you implement what you have learned into your life?

Has this book inspired you to look into other books? Which ones?

Are there any quotes from the book you would like to remember? Write them here.

Oak Tree Reading Workbook

Tiny Habits

BJ Fogg

All Discussion Questions

Introduction Chapter

- What cultural message do we internalize about change?
- What is flawed in our approach to change?
- What does popular thinking about habit formation lead to?
- What three things should you do to design successful habits?
- What does not reliably change behavior on its own? What is the name of this fallacy?
- In what three ways can we create lasting change?
- How does the scarcity mindset affect our ability to change?
- Describe the Maui Habit.
- How does risk impact our ability to change?
- How does our aspiration culture negatively impact our ability to change?
- Which two components of behavioral change are unreliable?
- What is a key maxim of Behavior design?
- What does celebrating small successes teach you how to do?
- What is the anatomy of Tiny Habits?

Chapter 1

- What are the three elements of behavior?
- What is motivation?
- What is ability?
- What is a prompt?
- Draw the Fogg Behavioral Model graph.
- What happens when a behavior is prompted above the Action Line?
- What combination causes a behavior to be above or the below the Action Line?
- Where do habits fall on the Fogg Behavioral Model?
- When will people do a behavior if motivation is middling?
- What makes you less likely to do a behavior?
- How do motivation and ability work together?
- How does repetition affect behavior?

- What does it mean to say motivation and ability are "continuous variables?"
- How can you disrupt a behavior?
- What is the rule of reciprocity?
- What are the three steps for troubleshooting a behavior?
- What are the two purposes of observing the world with a Behavior Model lens?
- In which two scientific ways should you examine your own behavior?
- What does the Motivation Monkey do?

Chapter 2

- What two words are indicators that you are relying on motivation to drive change?
- What are the three sources of motivation?
- What are the four elements of motivation that make it hard to control?
- Why is motivation unreliable?
- Why don't aspirations yield results?
- What is the difference between aspirations, outcomes, and behaviors?
- When can you achieve aspirations and outcomes?
- What does the term "goal" usually indicate?
- Draw the Swarm of Behaviors tool.
- What question do you ask when creating a Swarm of Behaviors chart?
- What are the three ways NOT to find your best habit?
- What are the three steps in Behavior Design?
- What are the criteria of a Golden Behavior?
- Draw a Focus Map grid.
- What question is asked during the first round of focus mapping?
- What question is asked during the second round of focus mapping?
- What distinction can help you avoid judgement during the second round of focus mapping?
- What is Fogg Maxim #1?
- What is the purpose of a Focus Map?
- What is the last step of Focus Mapping?
- What should you think about your new habits as?

Chapter 3

- What assumption do most people operate under?
- Why are small changes better than big changes?
- What are the drawbacks of attempting big changes?
- What is the "burst and bust" cycle?
- What are the 4 steps in Behavior Design?
- Why do we want to make behaviors easy to do?
- How does ability affect behavior on the Behavioral Model graph?
- When you design a new habit, what are you designing for?
- What question should you always start with when creating a new habit? What is the name for this question?
- What are the 5 ability factors?
- Why is the Ability Chain a transformative tool?
- What makes a habit design unstable?
- What is the Breakthrough Question?
- What three things make behaviors easier to do?
- What is "skilling up"?
- When should you engage in skilling up?
- What is decision fatigue?
- What are the two ways to make a habit tiny?
- What is the objective of the Starter Step?
- What is an important part of the Tiny Habits mindset?
- Why does the Starter Step have a big impact?
- What is Scaling Back?
- How do you determine which step you should start with?
- What are the four questions in the Design Flow?
- How do you keep a habit alive?
- What feelings are a sign that your habit is not tiny enough?
- What is important to remember about procrastination?

Chapter 4

- What is crucial to know about the effect of prompts on behavior?
- What makes prompts an invisible driver of behavior?
- What are the 5 steps in behavior design?
- What two things will keep a behavior from happening?
- Why don't many prompts work?
- What are the three types of prompts?
- Why do person prompts often not work?
- What is a context prompt?
- What kind of behaviors are context prompts best suited for?

- If a prompt is not working, what should you do and not do?
- What is an action prompt?
- What type of prompt is the most useful?
- What is an Anchor?
- What is behavior sequencing?
- What creates a reliable habit?
- What is the Tiny Habit Recipe?
- List a few examples of anchors.
- What three things should you take into account when looking for a good anchor?
- Why is experimentation important in habit design?
- What is a Trailing Edge?
- What is a Meanwhile Habit?
- What is a Pearl Habit?
- How can a pearl habit help in situations where we feel powerless?
- How do people change best?

Chapter 5

- What do adults rarely do?
- What results from celebrating the Tiny Habits way?
- What two things define what celebration is?
- Why is celebration an important element of behavioral change?
- How does effective celebration affect the brain?
- How does celebration correlate with learning?
- What is the psychological definition of learning?
- What reinforces behavior?
- Aside from positive feelings, what is another type of positive experience?
- What is the relationship between dopamine and good feelings?
- What is reward prediction error?
- How do celebrations hack the reward prediction error?
- What is directly connected to how you feel when you do a behavior?
- How quickly can habits form when connected to strong positive emotions?
- What creates habits?
- What is the Spectrum of Automaticity?
- What causes a behavior to become more automatic each time you do it?
- What is the definition of a reward?
- When do rewards need to occur?

- What types of rewards are unhelpful when trying to create a new habit?
- What two factors are the dopamine reward reaction dependent on?
- What is Fogg Maxim #2?
- What are the 2 steps to help a habit root quickly?
- What will occur if your celebration feels phony?
- What is Shine?
- What is a Power Celebration?
- What are the three reasons you should celebrate after doing a tiny habit?
- What may be happening if you feel celebrating small stuff is hard for you?
- Why can digging deep help you discover the value of celebrating?
- What is the purpose of lowering your expectations?
- List a few strategies for cultivating the feeling of success.
- What is the fastest way to wire in a new habit?
- What two things are you training when you rehearse your tiny habits?
- What are the three times to celebrate a tiny habit?
- After you develop a habit, under what circumstances should you reimplement celebrations?
- What will cause your brain to rewire a habit to want to avoid it?
- What is the benefit of engaging in unplanned celebrations?
- Why do celebrations affect confidence?
- What is a celebration blitz?

Chapter 6

- Describe the garden metaphor for habits.
- How long does it take for habits to grow to their full expression?
- What three things does habit formation time depend on?
- What determines how difficult it is to form a habit?
- What are the two general categories of habits?
- Describe an example of a growing habit.
- What is the limitation of growing habits?
- What does a multiplying habit look like?
- What role do aspirations play in creating growth and multiplication habits?
- What doesn't matter very much in terms of success?
- What can happen when fear is removed?
- How do demotivators affect habits?

- Why is the first time you do a behavior critical?
- When can people do harder behaviors?
- How do you acquire the skills of change?
- What are the three steps of Behavior Crafting?
- What skill helps you go from tiny to transformative?
- What are three guidelines for behavior crafting?
- How will you feel when you are doing the right thing?
- What are the two components of Self-Insight?
- What are the three guidelines for self-insight?
- What kind of change should you look for?
- What three skills are associated with Process Skills?
- What is the Process Skill?
- What moves your comfort edge?
- List the 4 guidelines for adjusting the difficulty of a habit.
- Why are Context Skills important to develop?
- What is the Context Skill?
- What two questions guide you for developing context skills?
- What are the 4 guidelines for Context Skills?
- What are 4 skills associated with Mindset Skills?
- What is the Mindset Skill?
- What deeply rooted human drive can help cultivate habits?
- Write some examples of ways to utilize the Mindset Skill.
- List the 5 Skills of Change.

Chapter 7

- Name and define the three categories of habits.
- What language isn't helpful for changing bad habits?
- What is a better analogy for changing bad habits?
- Why does the inability to stop a habit cause shame?
- List the three steps in the Behavioral Change Masterplan.
- What type of habit should you focus on in Phase #1 and why?
- What is the benefit of starting with creating new behaviors first?
- What are the three components of a habit you can alter to stop a behavior?
- What is a common mistake when trying to stop a bad habit?
- Which of your specific habits should you start with when working towards changing a general habit?
- What are the three ways to address the prompt of a habit in order to stop a behavior?
- List the 5 factors in the Ability Chain and how you can use each of them in your favor to stop a habit.

- Why is starting with motivation a mistake when trying to stop a habit?
- What are the two options for decreasing motivation to stop a habit?
- What is a demotivator?
- What are the drawbacks to using demotivators?
- List the 4 ways you can scale back a change.
- Why does scaling back work?
- What will cause habit swapping to fail?
- What is prompt remapping?
- What can help if you find yourself forgetting to do the new habit?
- What visual aid can help you while designing a habit swap?
- What are the four options for swapping a habit?
- What are some options to try if your habit swap isn't working?
- What are habits of omission?

Chapter 8

- What is a powerful driver of behavior?
- Why is it important to get cooperation when you are designing change?
- What maxim helps influence others to change their behaviors?
- What can open other people up to new types of change?
- When are we influencing the behavior of others?
- What makes change harder for others in the future?
- What two things must you do in order to help others change?
- What are the two approaches for getting others to change?
- What is the first step in designing change in a group?
- What is the second step in designing change in a group?
- What is the objective of the second step?
- Describe the process as a Ringleader for finding golden behaviors.
- Which question should the Ninja use for step 3?
- What is step 4 for designing change in a group?
- What question should a ringleader ask in step 4?
- In step 5, who should you talk to in order to find out what is successfully prompting a target behavior?
- What method helps other people feel successful?
- When should we offer positive feedback?
- What should we look for in response to giving positive feedback?
- When does feedback have the most emotional power?
- What should a ringleader do in step 7?

- Under what 4 categories can people fall when you are trying to design a behavioral change?
- What group(s) should you focus on and what group(s) should you not spend time on?
- What do innovators often do wrong with respect to these 4 groups?

Oak Tree Reading Workbook

Tiny Habits

BJ Fogg

Complete Vocab List

Behest:

Berate:

Dubious:

Forebode:

Intractable:

Iterate:

Nefarious:

Perpetuate:

Pragmatic:

Profuse:

Referendum:

Oak Tree Reading Workbook

Tiny Habits

BJ Fogg

Complete Key Terms List

ABC of Tiny Habits:

Ability:

Action Line:

Action Prompt:

Anchor:

B=MAP:

Behavior Crafting:

Breakthrough Question:

Context Prompt:

Context Skill:

Discovery Question:

Focus Map:

Fogg Behavioral Model:

Fogg Maxim #1:

Fogg Maxim #2:

Golden Behavior:

Growth Habit:

Magic Wanding:

Mindset Skill:

Motivation:

Multiplication Habit:

PAC:

Person Prompt:

Power Celebration:

Process Skill:

Prompt:

Scaling Back:

Self-Insight:

Shine:

Spectrum of Automaticity:

Starter Step:

Swarm of Behaviors:
100

Tiny Habit Recipe:

Trailing Edge:

Final Reflections Page

Use this space to write out your final thoughts, opinions, ideas, or feelings about your experience reading this book. This will help you later when you want a refresher on the material.

We hope you found this resource useful and look forward to helping you again soon for your next read.

About The Author

Oak Tree Reading creates comprehensive workbooks for your favorite non-fiction books. Primary genres include self-help, communication, relationships, and professional skills.

Our workbooks have been carefully designed to optimize learning. This allows you to get the most from what you are reading.

Read with friends. Our workbooks are perfect for facilitating meaningful discussions in any type of group setting. They are a great resource for educators, as well. Try it out! Soon you won't want to read any other way.

Sign up for our newsletter for updates on the latest releases at https://www.oaktreereading.com.

Leave Us A Review!

Did you enjoy this workbook? Please consider leaving us a review!

Your feedback tells us if we are doing a good job and helps us find ways to improve. Reviews and ratings help other people find our workbooks, too.

We appreciate your support!

Made in the USA
Middletown, DE
11 November 2023

42440429R00060